The Clever Carp

by **Cath Jones**

illustrated by
Kurnia Dewi Hernawan

Jill's gran was a fishing champ!

She had a long rod and the best boat.

"Can I be a fishing champ too?" Jill said.

"Yes," said Gran. "Hop in!"

They set off to catch a BIG fish.

Chug, chug, chug.

They went up the river.

"There's a clever, old carp in this river," said Gran.

"Let's catch it!" said Jill.

They put bait on a hook.

Now we wait.

Quick as a flash, the carp dashed out.

It crept under the boat.

It bit the bait.

"Gran!" said Jill.

"Hold on tight!" said Gran.

The carp swam off with a flip-flap

of its tail.

It took Jill and Gran for a spin.

The boat went up and down the river.

"This is fun!" said the carp.

When the carp let go, Jill did not mind.

"I had fun with that old fish!"
said Jill.

"I do not want to catch it!"
said Jill. "Thank you, carp."

The carp swam off with
a flip-flap of its tail.

That was Jill and Gran's last fishing trip...

...but not their last boat trip.

Quiz

1. Jill's gran was a fishing _____.
a) Winner
b) Rod
c) Champ

2. The carp is...
a) Silly
b) Clever
c) Funny

3. What did Jill and Gran put
on the hook?
a) Fish
b) Bait
c) A hat

4. I had _____ with that old fish!

a) Fun

b) A picnic

c) A hug

5. That was Jill and Gran's last _____ trip.

a) Fishing

b) Carp

c) Boat

Turn over for answers

Book Bands for Guided Reading

The Institute of Education book banding system is a scale of colours that reflects the various levels of reading difficulty. The bands are assigned by taking into account the content, the language style, the layout and phonics. Word, phrase and sentence level work is also taken into consideration.

Maverick Early Readers are a bright, attractive range of books covering the pink to white bands. All of these books have been book banded for guided reading to the industry standard and edited by a leading educational consultant.

Pink
Red
Yellow
Blue
Green
Orange
Turquoise
Purple
Gold
White

To view the whole Maverick Readers scheme, visit our website at
www.maverickearlyreaders.com

Or scan the QR code above to view our scheme instantly!

Quiz Answers: 1c, 2b, 3b, 4a, 5a